300 Incredible Things for Kids on the Internet

VIP Publishing
Marietta, Georgia • (800) 909-6505
Distributed by M.K. Distributors, Inc.

ISBN 0-9658668-1-5

Introduction

The Internet is an infinite encyclopedia of information and resources, but much of it, frankly, is not worth your time. I have written this book to help you take advantage of sites that will be valuable and interesting to you. Computers and the Internet are meant to be educational, useful and fun. This book should help you have those experiences. Happy surfing and learning.

Ken Leebow
Leebow@News-letter.com
http://this.is/TheLeebowLetter

About the Author

Ken Leebow has been in the computer business for over 20 years. The Internet has fascinated him since he began exploring its riches a few years ago, and he has helped thousands of individuals and businesses understand and utilize its resources.

When not on the Net, you can find Ken playing tennis, running, reading or spending time with his family. He is living proof that being addicted to the Net doesn't mean giving up on the other pleasures of life.

— Dedication —

To my Mom, who as PTA president 40 years ago wrote the following wise words:

For a happier New Year for all of us and our children, let us try to resolve...

To help our children learn from example rather than from admonition or precepts. To visit school more often and learn about our children, their successes and their occasional frustrations, their teachers and the changing educational practices, so that we may offer the understanding, patience, and love they need to live and learn effectively.

To avoid placing premature and unreasonable pressure on our children for achievement. To try to avoid substitution for our own precious time. Buying expensive gifts and giving elaborate parties is no substitute for a parent's time and attention.

And above all, avoiding compromise for social status, to hold our values high for a happier and rewarding life between us and our children.

—Joan Leebow

Acknowledgments

Putting a book together requires many expressions of appreciation. I do this with great joy, as there are several people who have played vital roles in the process:

- My kids, Alissa and Josh, who helped identify some of the cool sites.

- My wife, Denice, who has been patient with me while I have spent untold hours on the Internet.

- Paul Joffe and Janet Bolton, of *TBI Creative Services*, for their editing and graphics skills and for keeping me focused.

- The multitude of great people who have encouraged and assisted me via e-mail, particularly Kristina Runciman, who serves as copy editor of my weekly e-mail newsletter.

- Mark Krasner and Janice Caselli for sharing my vision of the book and helping make it a reality.

TABLE OF CONTENTS

TABLE OF CONTENTS (continued)

CHAPTER I
FOR PARENTS

1
Trash on the Net

http://www.surfwatch.com
http://www.netnanny.com
http://www.cyberpatrol.com
These software products can help keep the "bad stuff" off your computer screen.

2
Parent Time

http://pathfinder.com/ParentTime
Parenting is never easy; let ParentTime assist.

3
Be Safe

http://www.safewithin.com
Safety is the issue at this site: auto, child, home, pet, travel and more.

4
Web Novice

http://www.webnovice.com
http://www.pbs.org/uti
http://edweb.sdsu.edu/edfirst/courses/webcue.html
There are many people who are new to the Net. Check out these sites for help.

5
American Council for Drug Education

http://www.acde.org
Let's get educated about this difficult problem area.

6
Parent's Place

http://www.parentsplace.com
This site says, "We operate under the belief that parents are the best resource for other parents."

7
Arrive Alive
http://www.ittautomotive.com/drivesafer
This one has a lot of good information and sobering statistics to help promote road safety.

8
The School Report
http://www.nsrs.com
An amazing source for statistical information about SAT scores by school, this site also has maps and other information about each school.

9
Smoke Free Kids
http://www.tobaccofreekids.org
Here are a couple of scary stats from this site: "Three thousand children start smoking every day; one third will eventually die from their addiction."

10
ParentSoup

http://www.parentsoup.com
All parents have been in hot water; let ParentSoup bail you out.

11
Attention Deficit Hyperactivity Disorder

http://www.nimh.nih.gov/publicat/adhd.htm
http://www4.interaccess.com/add
http://www.chadd.org
If you can say all that, you don't have it. Need to know more about ADD? Check out some great resources at these sites.

12
Family Education

http://www.familyeducation.com
A site dedicated to helping parents take an active role in their kids' education.

13
Kid Gift Time

http://www.kidtools.com
If you need a great site to research or buy an educational product, this is it. The age range is 0–12.

14
Entertainment Software Rating Board

http://www.esrb.com
Check out the ratings for software games here. It will also tell you the age groups that the games are designed for.

15
Baseball Parent

http://users.aol.com/baseparent
Mom and apple pie go well with this site. If you're a baseball parent, this one's a hit.

16
Multiculturalism
http://curry.edschool.virginia.edu/go/multicultural
Multiculturalism is becoming a big part of our education system and school curriculum. Read and learn all about it here.

17
Can We Get Along?
http://www.rosemond.com/parenting
I've enjoyed John Rosemond's perspective; I hope you will too. His parental advice is straightforward and makes a lot of sense.

18
The Gifted Child
http://www.gifted-children.com
Have an especially bright child? Check out this site that is meant for gifted kids and parents.

19
The Department of Education
http://www.ed.gov/Picks/97
Yep, the DOE even has a hotlinks section that will provide you with some interesting sites to see. Click on the "Picks o' the Month" section.

20
National PTA
http://www.pta.org
You have probably been paying the dues for years. So, visit the site and use the PTA's resources.

21
KidsHealth
http://www.ama-assn.org/KidsHealth
The American Medical Association provides a wealth of information about children's health. Go for a checkup.

CHAPTER II
LOOK IT UP

22
Encarta Online

http://encarta.msn.com/EncartaHome.asp

This is Microsoft's encyclopedia online. Check out the school house and quiz.

23
Internet Guide

http://www.ebig.com

http://nobel.eb.com

Encyclopedia Britannica wants to make being on the Net a little easier. Check out its Internet Guide. And as a bonus: Look at its Nobel Prize winner's site.

24
Encyclopedia Internet
http://www.cs.uh.edu/~clifton/micro.a.html
The Net really is an encyclopedia, but it is not categorized as such. This is no easy task, but here is a site that does a good job.

25
Chemistry Encyclopedia
http://www.scimedia.com/chem-ed/scidex.htm
Look up hundreds of terms and concepts; pictures are included at no charge.

26
Dictionaries
http://www.m-w.com
http://www.dictionary.com
The well-known Webster's dictionary is on the Net. It even has a "word for the day" section.

27
Thesaurus
http://www.thesaurus.com
Sounds like some kind of dinosaur, but Roget's is online for your assistance.

28
Dictionaries
http://www.bucknell.edu/~rbeard/diction.html
Many more than you might have dreamed available.

29
One Look
http://www.onelook.com
You will, no doubt, look at this site more than once. It has over 50 excellent dictionaries in different disciplines. Check it out on the Net.

30
A, B, C...Z

http://www.enchantedlearning.com/Dictionary.html
http://www.littleexplorers.com/Letters.html
These are fun dictionaries for the young members of the family. They present an engaging learning experience for the parent and child.

31
Technology Dictionary

http://www.currents.net/resources/dict/dictionary.html
Find out about emoticons, country domain names and HTML stuff.

32
<u>Search the Net</u>

http://www.altavista.digital.com

http://www.infospace.com

http://www.infoseek.com

http://www.yahoo.com

http://www.hotbot.com

http://www.lycos.com

http://www.excite.com

http://www.search.com

http://www.askjeeves.com

http://www.isleuth.com

http://home.microsoft.com/access/allinone.asp

If you can't find it in this book, make sure you check out some of the best search engines on the Net.

33
Going Searching
http://www.search.com/Alpha/1,6,0,0200.html
Search.com has an A to Z listing of sites that allow you to search for just about anything.

34
Find an Old Friend (or a new one)
http://www.four11.com
http://www.whowhere.com
http://www.bigfoot.com
http://www.switchboard.com
http://www.theultimates.com
Find anyone's e-mail address by using these information search engines.

35
E-mail Research Assistance

http://www.dejanews.com
http://www.reference.com
http://www.liszt.com
These sites let you look up newsgroup and mailing list information.

36
Newspaper Article Search Engine

http://www.nytimes.com/search/daily
New York Times

http://167.8.29.8/plweb-cgi/ixacct.pl
USA Today

http://www.washingtonpost.com/wp-srv/searches/mainsrch.htm
Washington Post

http://www.LATimes.com/HOME/ARCHIVES/simple.htm
Los Angeles Times

37
Worldwide Newspapers

http://www.naa.org/hot
http://newo.com/news
http://www.ecola.com/news/press
http://www.newslink.org
http://www.voyager.co.nz/~vag118/news.html
http://www.mediainfo.com/ephome/npaper/nphtm/online.htm
http://www.all-links.com/newscentral

You'll probably need certain newspaper articles for reports. Here are listings of papers from all over the world.

38
Tomorrow Morning

http://morning.com

Tomorrow Morning is a weekly newspaper for kids 8 to 14. It's designed to motivate kids to read, become more involved in the world around them and more easily understand the issues that affect their lives.

"I found something really gross and disgusting
on the Internet—my school lunch menu!"

39
Research Papers
http://www.researchpaper.com
We all have to do them. This is the place to get a lot of help with your papers.

40
Kathy Schrock
http://www.capecod.net/schrockguide
An educator, Kathy has a simple and informative page for kids, teachers and parents. Using slide shows, she helps make the Internet easier.

41
Ask an Expert
http://www.askanexpert.com/askanexpert
Go ahead; ask these experts a question.

42
Homework Helper
http://idea.startribune.com
This is the newspaper from Minneapolis. It has a great current events quiz that changes daily, a Q&A section by subject area and some good links.

43
The Internet Schoolhouse
http://www.internetschoolhouse.com
This is an excellent site that has information on just about any subject. Check it out; you'll be glad you attended.

44
B.J. Pinchbeck's Homework Helper
http://tristate.pgh.net/~pinch13/index.html
B.J. says: "If you can't find it here, then you just can't find it!" He has one heck-of-a site. By the way, he is eleven years old.

45
My Virtual Reference Desk
http://www.refdesk.com
The Internet is the worlds largest library, containing millions of books, artifacts, images, documents, maps, etc. This site will help you find it all.

46
The Library of Congress
http://lcweb.loc.gov
This library is mammoth and rich with information. Check it out and see what information you can use. I'm sure you will visit here frequently.

47
Ask ERIC
http://ericir.syr.edu
ERIC actually stands for Educational Resources Information Center. This is a federally-funded, national information system that provides a variety of services and products on a broad range of education-related issues.

48
The Digital Librarian
http://www.servtech.com/public/mvail/home.html
This is a librarian's choice of the best of the Web.

49
School Isn't Out Here
http://www.cyberschoolmag.com
Educators, families and surfers will find exciting new articles and thousands of excellent resources to make learning exciting and fun.

50
Why?
http://whyfiles.news.wisc.edu/oldstorylist.html
Do you frequently ask "why?" If so, go to the Why Files. You'll be happy you did; and don't ask me why!

51
The Internet Public Library

http://www.ipl.org
You will find a lot of resource information at this site. It even has a section for youth and teens.

52
Biography

http://www.biography.com
This site has over 18,000 biographies of famous people. Search for a well-known name, and it will be there.

53
Online Educator

http://ole.net/ole
If you want to brown-nose your teacher, tell him or her about this site, and make sure you go to the "Search our Archives" sections. Of course, it will be a good resource for you, too.

54
Cornell's Arts and Social Science Gateway

http://www.tc.cornell.edu/Edu/ArtSocGateway

Get to the gate. Maybe you'll do so well in school that this path will lead you to Cornell.

55
Information at Your Fingertips

http://info-s.com

This site has over 30,000 links. It is well organized and will probably provide you with a world of good information. Take it for a spin and get acquainted with it.

56
Cliffs Notes

http://www.cliffs.com

You know them well, and this is a well-designed site. There is some great information, and it's a fun site to visit.

57
Yahoo! U
http://www.yahoo.com/promotions/b2s97/onsale.html
Yes, that is the name of this site. You will find tons of good information here.

58
Yahoo! for Kids
http://www.yahooligans.com
When it comes to knowing where to find things on the Net, Yahoo! is one of the leaders. See what sites it recommends for you.

59
Pathfinder for Kids
http://pathfinder.com/kids
http://pathfinder.com/SIFK
http://pathfinder.com/TFK
Pathfinder is Time/Warner on the Net. Sports Illustrated, Time magazine and the kids sites have interesting and timely information.

60
It's a Kid's World

http://www.pbs.org/kids
http://home.miningco.com/kids
This one will be sure to delight kids and teens. It has interesting sites, changes on a regular basis and has educational information such as "kid science."

61
Family Friendly

http://www.virtuocity.com/family.html
Go ahead and search for "family friendly" sites from this location. Just about any area of interest is covered.

62
Komando

http://www.komando.com
Kim Komando, a computer radio personality, has an excellent Web site. It is well designed, and you will find a lot of great resource information. Kim understands that too much information can be a bad thing; she gives you just enough.

63
Education Index
http://www.educationindex.com/lifestage.html
http://www.educationindex.com/education_resources.html
Get an index of sites that are age appropriate—from prenatal to careers. Or you can take a look at it by category.

64
Web Treasures for Students
http://www.edsoasis.org/Treasure/Treasure.html
This site is organized by school subject area, and you will find a few treasures here. This is also a good site to show to your teacher.

65
Turner, IBM and Education
http://www.solutions.ibm.com/k12
http://learning.turner.com
Turner and IBM have interesting educational sites for grades K– 12.

66
Lycos and AOL Knows Kids

http://www.lycos.com/kids
http://www.aol.com/netfind/kids
Lycos and AOL make it a little easier for kids on the Net.

67
Children's Express

http://www.ce.org
At this site, you will find information and news for kids. Serious and fun things
are there for you.

68
4Kids

http://www.4kids.org
Younger kids will have fun exploring all the neat places at this site. Wait for a
rainy day; you'll be here for hours (maybe days).

69
Surfing the Net With Kids
http://www.surfnetkids.com/feldman

Barbara Feldman, a columnist, has interesting things for kids to do on the Net.

70
Have Fun and Learn at Beakman.com
http://www.beakman.com

Beakman's motto: "A good question is a very powerful thing." A fun place for kids of all ages to learn. Great graphics!

71
CyberBee
http://www.cyberbee.com

From great clip art to other great educational sites on the Web, Linda (the bee), has them for you.

72
Virtual Classroom
http://www.whc.net/KCOS/class.html
Art, health, science, math and more. This site has many resources for your studies.

73
Schools on the Net
http://web66.coled.umn.edu/schools.html
What schools are on the Net? Web66 will let you know.

74
The Electronic Newstand
http://www.enews.com/channel/0, 1026, 15,00.html
This site has tons of stuff for all the family members. Check it out and plan on staying for awhile.

75
We're All Kids
http://www.kidscom.com
While you might think this site is for the younger kids, forget it. Find out about holidays, the heart and tons of other stuff here. It's for the kid in all of us.

76
Kids Linking Around the World
http://www.kidlink.org
This is a world where kids can join together and talk. This organization joins kids from the ages of 10–15 together for a global dialogue.

77
Do Your Homework!
http://www.schoolsucks.com
If you occasionally forget to do your work, this site can help during those times.

78
Young Bucks

http://www.younginvestor.com
Monetary issues for teenagers. Learn about financial matters while you're young.

79
Kid's Bank

http://www.kidsbank.com
Interesting money facts and calculators. Adults might even learn a thing or two.

80
Everything Cool Magazine

http://www.everythingcool.com
Movies, music, sports and video games. "Everything Cool" is a great place to visit for teens looking for interesting information online.

81
TeenVoices

http://www.teenvoices.com
A teen magazine written by teens for teens.

82
The Last Word

http://www.last-word.com
How does a potato-powered clock work? Find out at this site. There are over 365 answers to a lot of interesting questions.

83
From Kids to Teens

http://www.cyberkids.com
http://www.cyberteens.com
These two sites have you covered from pre-teen through your teenage years.

84
ThinkQuest

http://library.advanced.org

This is an educational adventure, which encourages students around the world to build Web pages. It represents a new model for learning and teaching. Most subject areas are covered.

85
The Brown Nose Department

http://www.thejournal.com/2hot/cool.html

http://www.education-world.com

Tell your teachers to go to the above sites, and you'll win a few brownie points. Just don't tell your friends; it's our secret.

CHAPTER III
LANGUAGE AND LITERATURE

86
English 101

http://www.grammarnow.com
http://www.columbia.edu/acis/bartleby/strunk
http://www.wsu.edu:8080/~brians/errors/errors.html
These sites will keep your grammar in check.

87
A Word a Day

http://www.wordsmith.org/awad/index.html
Get a new vocabulary word e-mailed to you every day. Go ahead, over 80,000 people do it!

88
Vocabulary University
http://www.vocabulary.com
Participate in these vocabulary puzzles to promote word mastery.

89
Irregardless
http://www.randomhouse.com/jesse/archive.cgi
http://www.word-detective.com
Is it a word? Well, check out Jesse's Word of the Day and find out about a lot of words. Also, the Word-Detective has some good ones for you.

90
A, B, C...
http://www.mcs.net/~kvj/spizz.html
Look for unusual words that have been used in top news stories.

91
Kids Publish on the Web

http://www.kidpub.org

KidPub is dedicated to letting kids express themselves. Posting stories on KidPub gives kids a planet-wide audience for their work. Over 11,000 stories are published at this site.

92
Samuel Langhorne Clemens

http://library.berkeley.edu/BANC/MTP

If you don't know who he is, then you need to visit this site. Tom and Huck are waiting for you.

93
Languages of the World

http://www.june29.com/HLP
http://www.sil.org/ethnologue

These sites provide a comprehensive catalog of language-related Internet resources. The first site has over 1,400 resources, and the other has 6,700 languages spoken in 228 countries.

94
Language Translation

http://www.logos.it/query.html
http://dictionaries.travlang.com

Have a word translated into many languages.

95
Project Gutenberg

http://www.promo.net/pg

Gutenberg invented the printing press. Michael Hart invented this idea of placing all books ever written, that are in the public domain, on the Internet.

CHAPTER IV
MATH AND SCIENCE

96
Cornell's Math and Science Gateway
http://www.tc.cornell.edu/Edu/MathSciGateway
Cornell will provide you with some great resources for the K–12 age group.

97
Flash Cards
http://www.wwinfo.com/edu/flash.html
Yep, flash cards are on the Net. This site allows you to customize it for the student's level.

98
Math Resource Center
http://forum.swarthmore.edu/math.topics.html
This is a great site for the student (K–College) and the teacher.

99
Conversion Calculators

http://www.worldwidemetric.com/metcal.htm
http://www.cchem.berkeley.edu/ChemResources/temperature.html
http://www.megacalculator.com/_Conv/mc_list.htm

You'll thank me for this one. U.S. citizens seem to have a problem converting to the metric system and from Fahrenheit to Celsius. Just go to these sites, and these problems will disappear.

100
Math, Math and More Math

http://www.erols.com/bram

This site has math for all ages and a tremendous number of links to other sites. Also, check out the section that gives quotations from famous mathematicians.

101
This Does Compute

http://homepage.interaccess.com/~wolinsky/measure.htm

Need a calculator? If it isn't at this site, it just doesn't add up.

102
Institute of Human Origins
http://www.zstarr.com/iho
Explore our origins. Plan on spending eons here.

103
Where Do Babies Come From?
http://www.olen.com/baby
The age-old question. This site is a must see for all (young and old).

104
Franklin Institute Science Museum
http://www.fi.edu/tfi/welcome.html
A museum and a lot more. While you're there, check out the educational hotlist.

105
Yuckie Sites for Kids
http://www.nj.com/yucky/index.html
A great place for science information and fun!

106
Mars: The Next Frontier
http://marsweb.jpl.nasa.gov
There is a lot of excitement about Mars. This site has updated pictures and much more. It's out of sight.

107
The Ocean
http://topex-www.jpl.nasa.gov
This project is for understanding our oceans and climate. Get this: It is done from space!

108
Science Surf
http://weber.u.washington.edu/~wcalvin/scisurf.html
William H. Calvin has an excellent science site with links to many other mind-expanding locations. If your thirst for knowledge is great, be prepared to stay awhile.

109
NASA in Cyberspace

http://www.nasa.gov
NASA is hip to your needs. It even has an area titled: "Cool NASA Websites."

110
Nine Planets

http://www.seds.org/nineplanets/nineplanets
That's how many there are in our solar system. At this site, learn everything you ever needed to know about the planets.

111
Windows to the Universe

http://www.windows.umich.edu
When it comes to understanding our universe, this is the place to visit. It even has explanations for: beginner, intermediate and advanced.

112
World Wildlife Fund

http://www.wwf.org
This is a beautiful site that will inform you about life on our planet and the sad extinction of many animals.

113
The Human Anatomy

http://www.innerbody.com
Get ready for a lot of pictures and descriptive information about the body.

114
The Science Learning Network

http://www.sln.org
Can anyone make science a great learning experience—fun, easy and informative? You bet, at the Science Learning Network.

115
Interactive Frog Dissection
http://curry.edschool.virginia.edu/go/frog/menu.html
This lab activity will help you learn the anatomy of a frog and also provide a better understanding of the anatomy of vertebrates, including humans.

116
Life on the Universe
http://www.lifeintheuniverse.com
Take a trip with Stephen Hawkings, and learn about the universe.

117
StarChild
http://starchild.gsfc.nasa.gov
The StarChild site is a service of the High Energy Astrophysics Science Archive Research Center (HEASARC). I promise this site is a lot easier to use than the name implies. This is a great site to learn about our solar system, universe and other space stuff.

"I tapped into the school's computer and changed all my grades. Then the school tapped into my computer and changed all my games to educational programs!"

118
The Wizard's Lab

http://library.advanced.org/11924

Learn about motion, sound, light, energy, electricity and magnetism at this fun site. You'll want to take the quiz and find out more about the preceding items.

119
How Things Work

http://www.phys.virginia.edu/Education/Teaching/HowThingsWork

Did you ever wonder how some of the things we take for granted work? Well, wonder no more.

120
Earthquakes

http://www.crustal.ucsb.edu/ics/understanding

Take a quiz and learn a lot about earthquakes at this site.

121
Volcano World

http://volcano.und.nodak.edu
http://vulcan.wr.usgs.gov
If it has anything to do with volcanoes, you will find it here.

122
Dinosaur-o-mania

http://www.dinosociety.org
Everyone is into dinosaurs; visit the society. Get lots of information, and check out the links page.

123
E=MC²

http://www.sas.upenn.edu/~smfriedm/einstein.html
Everything you ever wanted to know about Albert Einstein. Okay, more than you wanted to know.

124
Junk Science

http://www.junkscience.com
I know it's hard to believe that anyone would try to fool us about scientific studies, but I promise you it happens. Don't be fooled again.

CHAPTER V
GEOGRAPHY AND MAPS

125
National Geographic

http://www.nationalgeographic.com

The famed foundation is now online. If you enjoy its detailed reporting on nature, science and the world around us, do not miss this site.

126
Geo Globe

http://library.advanced.org/10157

Play a geography game at this site. You choose the level: beginner to advanced.

127
Ain't No Mountain High Enough

http://www.inch.com/~dipper/highpoints.html

http://www.inch.com/~dipper/world.html

Find out the tallest elevation in each state and around the world.

128

Library of Congress Studies Countries

http://lcweb2.loc.gov/frd/cs/cshome.html

Get detailed information on most countries at this site.

129

It Takes a Village

http://www.geocities.com/Athens/Forum/1910/wvp.html

What if there were only 1,000 people in the world? What would the statistical breakdown be? Here are the facts.

130

Can We All Get Along?

http://www.iearn.org

The International Education and Resource Network enables young people to tackle projects designed to make a meaningful contribution to the health and welfare of the planet and its people.

131
Flags of the World
http://flags.mmcorp.com
Need a flag and other basic information about a country? Check this site out.

132
This is Geography
http://members.aol.com/bowermanb/101g.html
This is a very nice resource for many geographic issues.

133
Country Information
http://www.city.net/countries
If you need information on any country, state or city, check out City.net's detailed resources.

134
State Web Sites

http://www.globalcomputing.com/states.html
Each state has its own Web site. Check them out to see what information they provide.

135
Countries Online

http://www.atlapedia.com/online/contents.htm
http://www.theodora.com/wfb/abc_world_fact_book.html
These sites contain key information about every country of the world—facts and data on geography, climate, people, religion, language, history and economy.

136
A World of Information

http://www.emulateme.com
Here's a world encyclopedia with flags, maps and more. And you can even listen to the national anthem of each country.

137
Get Help from the CIA
http://www.odci.gov/cia/publications/nsolo/wfb-all.htm
If you're doing a project about any country, the CIA would like to assist you.

138
States Online
http://www.scvol.com/States
http://www.piperinfo.com/state/states.html
http://govinfo.kerr.orst.edu
Get a lot of information about states at these sites.

139
The United Nations
http://www.un.org
http://www.pbs.org/tal/un
Every school kid can now say: "I have been to the United Nations."

140
Let's Go to the Park
http://www.nps.gov
http://www.llbean.com/parksearch
Some of our national treasures are at these sites.

141
Great Maps
http://www.nationalgeographic.com/resources/ngo/maps
http://pathfinder.com/Travel/maps/index.html
Let National Geographic and Pathfinder show you the way. These sites show almost every country in the world. Bookmark it for those school projects.

142
Maps in the News
http://www-map.lib.umn.edu/news.html
Talk about current events. If you need a map of an area that is currently in the news, no doubt this site will have it.

143
Where in the World?

http://www.astro.ch/atlas

If you need to know where any city in the world is located, this is the place to go.

144
Family Trip

http://www.delorme.com/cybermaps/cyberrouter.htm

http://www.freetrip.com

http://www.mapsonus.com

Getting in the car to go somewhere? Maybe a vacation? Check out these three sites to get great directions for your trip.

145
Driving Directions

http://www.zip2.com

Do you need to get good directions to a friend's house? This site will get you door-to-door, and a map comes with it.

CHAPTER VI
HISTORY, POLITICS AND GOVERNMENT

146
History Net
http://www.thehistorynet.com
When it comes to history, this site has it all.

147
World History
http://we.got.net/docent/scwriter.htm
Guaranteed to have a world of information. Each country has a listing with links galore.

148
An Abridged History of the United States
http://www.us-history.com
This author wants all students to have an understanding of our history.

149
History 102
http://hum.lss.wisc.edu/hist102
Get a good dose of American history from the Civil War to the present.

150
How the West was Found
http://www.pbs.org/lewisandclark
Travel back in time with Lewis and Clark.

151
Ancient Sites
http://www.ancientsites.com
Ancient history comes alive at this site. There is a Virtual Classroom Program designed to create a worldwide learning community focused on history.

152
World Heritage
http://www.unesco.org/whc/heritage.htm
The Galapagos, Grand Canyon and over 500 other sites. These cultural and natural sites constitute a common heritage, to be treasured as unique testimonies to an enduring past.

153
Egyptology
http://www.kv5.com
Go to the Theban Mapping Project to live, learn and feel the excitement of the archaeological digs going on in Egypt.

154
The History Channel
http://www.historychannel.com
Where the past comes alive…online.

155
History at a Glance

http://www.hyperhistory.com

This is an interesting way to present the history of the world.

156
World Wars

http://www.worldwar1.com

http://www.worldwar2.com

The wars to end all wars. Well, not exactly, but here are two sites to educate you about WWI & II.

157
Benjamin Franklin

http://www.fi.edu/TOC.franklin.html

If you ever need to do a report on Benjamin Franklin, or just want to know more about the man on the one hundred-dollar bill, this site will do it.

158
Abraham Lincoln
http://www.netins.net/showcase/creative/lincoln.html
Honest Abe has been done proud at this site. There are tons of resources for you here.

159
U.S. Civil War
http://www.uscivilwar.com
Get detailed information about the war, and visit links that will take you to other sites.

160
Early America
http://www.earlyamerica.com
At this site you'll find a magazine, pictures, historical documents and more.

161
<u>In 1492, Columbus Sailed the Ocean Blue</u>
http://sunsite.unc.edu/expo/1492.exhibit/Intro.html
Columbus may be less politically correct in the 90s, but here is a site that has a lot of information about him and his travels.

162
<u>Art Online</u>
http://witcombe.bcpw.sbc.edu/ARTHLinks.html
http://kultur-online.com/finesite
There is a lot of conversation about art being taken out of the schools, but it is in full bloom on the Net.

163
<u>Famous Speeches</u>
http://www.audionet.com/speeches
From Roosevelt to Bush, you can listen to many famous orations.

"Does anybody use the computers at your high school?
I accidentally e-mailed them your diary."

164
Historical Biographies
http://www.tiac.net/users/parallax
There are over 18,000 searchable historical figures at this site. Make sure you take the "Master Biographer Challenge."

165
Those Were the Days
http://www.scopesys.com/today
http://www.440.com/twtd/today.html
http://www.mrshowbiz.com/dailydose
http://www.historychannel.com/thisday
http://www.thehistorynet.com/today/today.htm
http://lcweb2.loc.gov/ammem/today/archive.html
What happened today in history? You will definitely find out here.

166
Three Branches of Government
http://www.erols.com/irasterb/gov.htm
This is the ultimate site about the U.S. government.

167
Core Documents of the USA
http://www.access.gpo.gov/su_docs/dpos/coredocs.html
From the Bill of Rights to Supreme Court decisions, you can find it all here.

168
Your Congress
http://thomas.loc.gov
In the spirit of Thomas Jefferson, this is a service of the U.S. Congress through its library. There is a lot of congressional and political information here.

169
Your Government Wants You

http://www.uncle-sam.com
http://www.fedstats.gov

There is information galore awaiting you at the above sites. Whether you are doing a project or just want to learn a lot, you can hang out here for quite awhile.

170
Mr. President

http://sunsite.unc.edu/lia/president
http://www.peoples.net/~southbd
http://www.grolier.com/presidents/preshome.html
http://www.pbs.org/presidents
http://www.columbia.edu/acis/bartleby/inaugural

Every President is listed at these sites. And as a bonus, check the last site: every inaugural speech ever given.

171
The White House

http://www.whitehouse.gov
http://www.whitehouse.gov/WH/kids/html/home.html
Everyone should make a trip to Washington, D.C. to see the White House. If you can't get there today, this is the next best thing.

172
Electoral College

http://www.bga.com/~jnhtx/ec/ec.html
Every four years we hear a lot about the Electoral College. This site allows you to "play" with the electoral process. Go ahead, pick a winner in each state and see what happens.

173
Politics on the Net

http://www.agora.stm.it/politic
This has political sites from around the globe. View the map, and click the part of the world interests you.

174
Leaders of the World

http://www.trytel.com/~aberdeen
http://www.geocities.com/Athens/1058/rulers.html

These sites list all the leaders of the world. If there is a Web site or e-mail address available, it is provided.

175
NARA

http://www.nara.gov

National Archives and Records Administration is the government agency responsible for overseeing the management of the records of the federal government. Lots of good stuff here; check the exhibit hall and the Internet resources.

CHAPTER VII
MUSEUMS AND ZOOS

176
Smithsonian Museum

http://www.si.edu/organiza/start.htm
While it might not be as rewarding as being there in person, it is only a click away.
At this site, you will be able to visit all of the different museums.

177
Art Appreciation

http://www.nga.gov
Art is alive and well at The National Gallery of Art. Go for a tour today.

178
Museum Guide

http://www.museumguide.com
Tell your folks you won't need to make a trip to the museum this weekend. And tell
them how much money you are saving them, since these museums are in Europe.

179
Museum USA
http://www.museumca.org/usa
The U.S. has a treasure trove of museums; go for a visit. There are no lines, and the admission is free.

180
Museums and More
http://www.dreamscape.com/frankvad/museums.html
This site presents over 200 museums, exhibits and other areas of special interest. Go ahead and take a guided tour.

181
ZooNet
http://www.mindspring.com/~zoonet
All the zoos in the land, and you won't have to deal with the smell.

182
The Electronic Zoo

http://netvet.wustl.edu/e-zoo.htm
Name the animal, and it's here. This site is educational and fun.

183
Free Willy

http://www.aquarium.org/keikohome.htm
This is the Web site of Keiko (of Free Willy movie fame). Check out the "live cam" in his 2-million gallon aquarium.

CHAPTER VIII
COLLEGE PREP

184
High Q

http://www.davideck.com

Okay, take the test(s) and show everyone how smart you are. You might want to take the tests in private first.

185
SAT Test

http://www.testprep.com

Take a sample SAT test online. There are other helpful resources at this site.

186
Your Best College Buy

http://www.pathfinder.com/money/colleges98

College is costly. Let this site assist you with figuring out the economic maze of going to college. Over 1,400 schools are evaluated.

187
Go College

http://www.gocollege.com
It would be hard to list all of the excellent things at this site. All I can say is: "Go there."

188
Just The Facts

http://www.memex-press.com/cc
Critical Comparisons is designed by education professionals and gives you the facts about colleges.

189
Internet College Exchange

http://www.usmall.com
Lots of information about colleges and assistance for the high school junior and senior. Check out and subscribe to the weekly e-mail newsletter.

190
The Center for All Collegiate Information
http://www.collegiate.net/infoi.html
This site merges the college and online worlds; a ton of information available here.

191
Locate a College Online
http://www.ecola.com/college
http://www-net.com/univ/list.html
http://www.clas.ufl.edu/CLAS/american-universities.html
http://www.universities.com
If a college is online, you'll find it here.

192
College Newspapers Online
http://www.all-links.com/newscentral/college
http://www.cpnet.com/college/newspapers.htm
Cuddle up to the screen and read a college newspaper. Not a bad way to get acquainted with a school.

193
What's It Gonna Cost?

http://www.salliemae.com/calculators/content.html

Let Sally Mae help you with understanding the cost of going to college.

194
College News

http://www.uwire.com

http://uwire.usatoday.com

A Northwestern student started this publication in 1994. Now it is considered a premier news source for college life. Learn about the issues on campus.

195
Financial Aid

http://www.finaid.org

Going to college? Want information about financial aid? This is your site.

196
Get the Edge

http://www.collegeedge.com
CollegeEdge has everything you need to prepare for college and your future. The site offers a college search tool, useful links, advice and guidance from an expert college panel.

197
Scholarships for All

http://www.fastweb.com
A great scholarship search engine. You will be able to find scholarship programs based on information you enter about your interests, experiences and family background.

198
CollegeFreshman

http://www.collegefreshman.com
An online e-zine for soon-to-be and current college newbies. At this site, you'll find college ratings, virtual campus tours, SAT schedules and financial aid tips.

199
College Bound?

http://www.collegeboard.org
http://www.ets.org
If college is on your agenda, then these are sites that you will want booked. From SATs to financial aid, it's here.

200
College

http://www.collegeview.com
Take a tour of over 3,500 colleges and universities. And there are lots of other goodies here for the college-bound.

201
Let's Review

http://www.review.com/college
If college is on your mind, then you will not want to miss The Princeton Review. Great info!

CHAPTER IX
PETS, HOBBIES AND SPORTS

202
Your Guide to Pets on the Net

http://www.acmepet.com
You can tell that they love pets at this site.

203
It's Raining Cats and Dogs

http://www.canismajor.com/dog
http://www.purina.com/Breeds_Profile
Before you go out and buy that cuddly puppy or furry animal, make sure you do a little research. These sites will let you know a lot about these great pets.

204
Keep that Pet Healthy

http://www.healthypet.com
Now that you have found your pet, here's a site that will help you keep it healthy.

"It's amazing what you can find on the Internet.
Here's a discussion group for left-handed short
people who like to collect autographed ear wax
from the pets of celebrity stunt doubles!"

205
The Animal Network
http://www.animalnetwork.com
http://www.allpets.com
Cats, dogs, fish, reptiles, horses and more.

206
The Path for Animal Lovers
http://petpath.com
PetPath is the place to find veterinary advice, learn more about your pet and other animals, converse with other pet owners and more.

207
What's In a Name
http://www.primenet.com/~meggie/petname.htm
Need a name for your new pet? Make a stop here to find one.

208
Animal Sounds

http://www.georgetown.edu/cball/animals/animals.html
And you thought animals all over the world sound the same? Find out how different they can be.

209
Something's Fishy

http://www.fishlinkcentral.com
This site is dedicated to promoting the aquarium hobby. Looks and sounds beautiful to me.

210
Youth Hockey

http://www.yhn.com/contents.htm
Hockey is a major sport for kids. This site will fill you in about kids on ice.

211
Little League Baseball
http://www.littleleague.org
Apple pie, Mom and Little League Baseball: All-American staples.

212
This Stuff Kicks
http://www.mlsnet.com/kidzone
Soccer has taken the country by storm. Check out Major League Soccer's kidzone.

213
I Wanna Be
http://www.tigerwoods.com
It seems like all kids (and adults) want to be Tiger Woods. Visit his official site.

214
Goin' Camping

http://www.campnetamerica.com
Have fun, and don't forget to pack this site as one of your tools.

215
Youth Sports on the Net

http://www.infosprts.com
Okay, kids, find out what is happening on the Net when it comes to sports.

216
Sport's Reporter

http://www.sportsline.com
http://www.foxsports.com
http://www.espn.com
http://www.cnnsi.com
If you are a big sports fan, you will want to make sure you visit these sites
frequently. It's not a hit; it's a grand slam!

CHAPTER X
MUSIC, MOVIES AND ENTERTAINMENT

217
RealAudio

http://www.realaudio.com

http://www.timecast.com

Some of the sites in this book are for your listening pleasure. You will need the RealAudio product to listen to them. So, go to this site and download the software. Yes, it is free. Then check out Timecast to learn about many of the great audio sites on the Net.

218
DeadRadio

http://www.deadradio.com

This is my favorite music on the Net. Listen to the Grateful Dead 24 hours day, seven days a week.

219
Listen Up

http://www.live-online.com
Listen to music on the Net. Sometimes it's live, and sometimes it's not.

220
Listen to Great Music

http://www.thedj.com/Main/thedj_web_radio.html
Every music type is covered here.

221
Music on the Net

http://www.rockonthenet.com
This is a great site that will keep you informed about all the great musicians and groups.

222
Music and Bands

http://www.unfurled.com

http://www.ubl.com

If you are looking for a band on the Net, make sure you go to Unfurled and the Ultimate Band List.

223
Country Music

http://countrysong.com

The most popular music in the U.S. If you like it, you'll not want to miss this site.

224
MTV and VH1

http://www.mtv.com

http://www.vh1.com

Cable music hits the Net.

225
Rolling Stone

http://www.rollingstone.com
This magazine has been reporting on music forever.

226
Concerts, Concerts, Concerts

http://www.pollstar.com
If you want to go to a concert, this is your site to find it.

227
CDs Galore

http://www.cdnow.com
If you like music, check out this spot. Find your favorite performer, and listen to clips from the album. Try before you buy.

228
Rock and Roll Hall of Fame

http://www.rockhall.com

The Net rocks at the Rock and Roll Hall of Fame.

229
Music Lyrics

http://www.lyrics.ch

This site has the words to over 40,000 songs in its inventory.

230
TV Guide

http://www.tvguide.com

http://www.tvguide.com/movies

This site is self-explanatory, but make sure you check out the movie section that has over 40,000 films listed. Don't forget to play the trivia game.

231
Movie Buff

http://www.moviebuff.net
That pretty much says it all. If you like movies, this is a site you will not want to miss.

232
Movies, Movies, Movies

http://www.moviefinder.com
http://us.imdb.com
http://allmovie.com
If you want to know about movies on the Net, these are your sites.

233
Movies Online

http://www.movieweb.com
A great site that links to Hollywood studios and has previews of current and future movies and more.

234
Box Office

http://www.boxoff.com

Going to the movies? Check out the reviews first.

235
What Time is That Movie Playing?

http://www.movielink.com

Now that you know all about movies, you need to know where they are playing in your town.

CHAPTER XI
FUN AND GAMES

236
Be My Buddy

http://www.aol.com

Send an instant message to friends who are online. America Online's excellent "Buddy List" software is available to anyone on the Net.

237
Chatting on the Net

http://www.yack.com
http://chat.yahoo.com

Chat rooms are one of the big areas on the Net. Go ahead, yack, yack, yack.

238
Bonus.com

http://www.bonus.com

The kids super site for fun. If you're a kid, go to this playground.

239
Dr. Suess

http://www.seussville.com
Kids of all ages love Dr. Suess, a classic of course.

240
Going Looney

http://www.nonstick.com
You'll go looney over this site. Hurry up, Bugs and friends aren't going to wait.

241
Gametime Help

http://www.segasages.com
http://www.thecheatersguild.com
Are you having a little trouble with one of your games? Let these sites assist you with winning them.

242
Sanrio

http://www.sanrio.com
If you know Hello Kitty, Keroppi or Pochacco, you must visit them on the Net. Of course, there are lots more friends waiting for you.

243
The Ultimate Origami Site

http://www.datt.co.jp/Origami
If you like Origami (the art of paper folding), you shouldn't miss this site. Notice the "jp" in the URL; this site is located in Japan.

244
Paintball

http://www.paintball.com
Do you love Paintball? At this site you can chat about it with other fans.

"My dad is afraid I'm turning into a computer weenie, so I told him I joined the trackball team."

245
Fun Facts
http://www.dreamsville.com/CSN/Wardo/fact.html
Have an interesting and fun fact e-mailed to you daily. For example, "Maine is the only state in the United States whose name has one syllable."

246
The Case Solve-it Mysteries
http://www.thecase.com
Use the Web, learn and have fun while you are challenging your critical thinking skills. Solve many of the mysteries at The Case.

247
Take the Challenge
http://www.quizmaster.com
Make sure you take the quiz about Coca-Cola. Yes, there are other quizzes here. Have some fun.

248
Games for Dummies
http://www.games.net
A very nice game site from the folks who bring you the "Dummy" books.

249
A&E Monthly Celebrity Trivia
http://mmnewsstand.com/Trivia
Questions about the famous people of our times, from John F. Kennedy to Madonna, Princess Diana to Mike Tyson.

250
SuperKids
http://www.superkids.com
Get unbiased reviews of children's software by parents, teachers and kids. There is also a lot of other cool stuff at this site. For example: a humor section.

251
DuJour

http://www.dujour.com
A fun-filled path to Internet Nirvana! Here you will find games and contests guaranteed to titillate, challenge and annoy.

252
What a Waste

http://www.amused.com
The site says it all: "Our hard-working experts have been exploring the Internet since long before it was trendy in their search for the Ultimate Guide to Wasting Time."

253
Crayola

http://www.crayola.com
Binney and Smith have assisted us all in being a kid. Now get to the coloring!

254
It's Game Time

http://www.happypuppy.com
This site has nothing to do with dogs. It is known to be one of the better sites for games. Have some fun.

255
Games Mania

http://www.gamesmania.com
I think the title says it all. Want to have some fun with games? Check it out.

256
April Fools

http://www.aprilfools.com
On the Net, enjoy April Fool's Day all year.

257
Come Play with Me

http://www.playsite.com
This site allows you to play chess, checkers or backgammon with other connected people. In the future, this will probably become a way of life. Check it out today.

258
You Must Be Joking!

http://listen.to/henny
Enjoy these timeless laughs from Henny Youngman, the King of One-Liners.

259
Student Net

http://www.student.net
If you want an archive of great crossword puzzles and to witness a group of creative college students, this Web site is a must see.

260
Headbone

http://www.headbone.com
Play some games, chat and other stuff at Headbone.

261
Send a Postcard or a Kiss

http://www.xenus.com/postcard
http://www.xenus.com/postcard/age.htm
http://www.thekiss.com/ekiss
Send a postcard for almost any occasion, even for a practical joke. And for that loved one, send a kiss.

262
E-Greeting Cards

http://www.sendgreeting.com
http://www.bytesizegreetings.com/cards.html
http://postcards.bookwire.com/greethings/send.greethings
http://www.marlo.com/card.htm
Go to these sites and send a greeting card. It's free, no postage required and it gets there instantly. And you get to use your creativity by writing the text on the card.

263
Virtual Flowers

http://www.virtualflowers.com/vflower_select.phtml
http://www.800florals.com/virtual
For Valentines Day, a birthday or maybe just a fun way to say, "I'm thinking of you." Send one of your friends some flowers.

264
Pinball Wizard
http://www.lysator.liu.se/pinball
Who would have thought—a comprehensive Web site about pinball?

265
Casper the Friendly Ghost
http://www.ghosts.org/links.html
Yep, there are ghosts even in cyberspace. This site has a lot of spooky stuff.

266
Lights, Camera, Action
http://www.earthcam.com
Crazy as it may seem, there are tons of cameras taking pictures all over the world. Find out where they are so you can be in on the action.

267
Everyone's Looking for Waldo
http://www.findwaldo.com
Go find Waldo.

268
License Plates of the World
http://danshiki.oit.gatech.edu/~iadt3mk/index.html
Ever play the game of looking for different state license plates when traveling?
This site has them from all over the world.

269
Driveways of the Rich and Famous
http://www.driveways.com
Robin Leach, watch out. All of us seem to be absorbed by these people, so check
it out on the Net.

270
CalendarLand

http://www.juneau.com/home/janice/calendarland

Five billion people on the planet, and we're all marking time! All kinds of interesting calendars.

271
It's Candy Time

http://www.candyusa.org

At this site, it sure is. Just don't tell your dentist.

272
Cookies Galore

http://www.cookierecipe.com

http://www.cookiegarden.com

Nothing better than the fresh smell of home baked cookies. Get some recipes here. And if you can't bake, just order them online.

273
The Cartoon Corner
http://www.cartooncorner.com
The fun starts here; learn how to draw cartoons. There are fun kids' quizzes, stories and more.

274
Trivia on the Net
http://www.trivia.net
If you are a trivia fan, check out Trivia.net. There are thousands of questions.

275
The Name Game
http://www.funster.com
Make words out of someone's name. It's fun, challenging and you play against the clock and other people. Show this site to your parents; they might like it too.

276
The Puzzle Depot
http://www.puzzledepot.com
Devoted to puzzles, board games, trivia, related books and software. You will find crosswords, riddles and word puzzles, logic and strategy software/board games and a large selection of shareware.

277
Puzzle Maker
http://www.puzzlemaker.com
Go ahead, spend hours here making your own puzzles. It's loads of fun and, of course, educational. Share this one with your teacher.

278
Two Ps
http://www.popsicle.com
http://www.pez.org
Not as tasty as the real things, but guaranteed not to make a mess.

279
What's Your Sign?

http://astrology.net
Astrology on the Net.

280
sdrawkcaB

http://smeg.com/backwards
Put in a URL and have the page read to you—backwards. This should drive your friends and family "yzarc."

281
Liven Up Your E-mail

http://st-www.cs.uiuc.edu/users/chai/figlet.html
http://users.inetw.net/~mullen/ascii.htm
http://www.info.polymtl.ca/ada2/tranf/www/asciiarts.html
When you send your friends and family an e-mail, put some fun text and art in the note.

282
FAO Schwarz

http://www.faoschwarz.com
Everyone feels like a kid at FAO Schwarz.

283
Dr. Toy

http://www.drtoy.com
Over 400 award winning toys and children's products are selected by Dr. Toy, fully described, with company phone numbers to call for more information.

284
Beanie Babies

http://www.ty.com
http://www.beaniemom.com
Nothing is hotter than Beanie Babies. Check out a complete listing and biography of all these critters.

285
Tamagotchi Lives

http://www.bandai.com

http://tamagotchi.cs1.com

If you don't know what Tamagotchi is all about, don't bother going here. But if you are one of the millions of people who have these "lovable" creatures, check it out.

286
The Limited

http://www.limited.com

Whether you are a kid or an adult, you probably wear some of the clothes. By the way, they own many of the stores that clothe America.

287
The Gap

http://www.gap.com

http://www.gapkids.com

You get to dress the Gap Kids on the Net. Kids love wearing Gap clothes, and they will have fun at this engaging site.

288
Disney, Disney, Disney
http://www.lido.com/disney
This isn't an official Disney site, but it will take you to a ton of Disney stuff. If you like Disney, plan on staying a couple of days. The good news: it's free.

289
Disney Secrets
http://www.hiddenmickeys.org/Secrets.html
All kinds of interesting stuff you never knew about Disney!

290
Disney Online
http://www.disney.com
http://www.family.com
http://www.disneyblast.com
http://www.disneybooks.com
The folks from Disney obviously enjoy and believe in the Net. If you like Disney offline, no doubt you'll enjoy it on the Net.

291
The Discovery Channel

http://www.discovery.com
http://school.discovery.com
Discovery has always made learning interesting, and it's no different on the Net. There is even a kid's section.

292
Warner Brothers

http://www.warnerbros.com
Where kids are king. Go have some fun.

293
Nickelodeon on the Net

http://www.nick.com
Nick is fun on TV and on the Net, too.

294
Fox Kids

http://www.foxkids.com

If you like the Fox TV shows, check out the fun they have in store for you.

CHAPTER XII
HOLIDAYS

295
Holiday Celebrations

http://www.holidays.net
Who doesn't love holidays? If it's on the Net, this site has it. Happy celebrating.

296
Happy Thanksgiving

http://www.night.net/thanksgiving
http://www.butterball.com
An Internet Thanksgiving. My times have changed.

297
Holidays Around the World

http://www.jpmorgan.com/cgi-bin/HolidayCalendar
http://www.classnet.com/holidays
These sites will allow you to find the holidays in any country.

298
Christmas Cards

http://www.ash.org.au/mmcard
Send a Christmas card to one of your loved ones. Make sure that they are on the Net.

299
What's Up, Santa?

http://www.northpole.com
http://www.claus.com
Any time of the year, you can have some fun at the North Pole. During the summer, chill out; during Christmas, well, just bring all the kids.

300
'Tis the Season

http://www.sidewalksanta.org
It's always better to give than receive. Have some fun and learn about this charitable organization.

List additional incredible things that you discover:

301

Site Name:

URL:

Comment:

302

SiteName:

URL:

Comment:

303

Site Name:

URL:

Comment:

304

Site Name:

URL:

Comment:

305

Site Name:

URL:

Comment:

306

Site Name:

URL:

Comment:

List additional incredible things that you discover (continued):

307

Site Name:

URL:

Comment:

310

Site Name:

URL:

Comment:

308

SiteName:

URL:

Comment:

311

Site Name:

URL:

Comment:

309

Site Name:

URL:

Comment:

312

Site Name:

URL:

Comment:

List additional incredible things that you discover (continued):

313

Site Name:

URL:

Comment:

314

SiteName:

URL:

Comment:

315

Site Name:

URL:

Comment:

316

Site Name:

URL:

Comment:

317

Site Name:

URL:

Comment:

318

Site Name:

URL:

Comment:

Index (by site number)

INDEX (BY SITE NUMBER)

INDEX (BY SITE NUMBER)

The Incredible Newsletter

If you are enjoying this book, you can also arrange to receive a steady stream of more "incredible Internet things," delivered directly to your e-mail address.

The Leebow Letter, Ken Leebow's weekly e-mail newsletter, provides new sites, updates on existing ones and information about other happenings on the Internet.

For more details about *The Leebow Letter* and how to subscribe, send an e-mail to:
Newsletter@Mindspring.com

Books by Ken Leebow

300 Incredible Things to Do on the Internet

300 Incredible Things for Kids on the Internet

300 Incredible Sports Sites on the Internet